TOILET MOUTH

Poems by Craig Podmore / 2016

Antiseptic

PRESS

First edition published by Antiseptic Press 2016

Copyright **Craig Podmore**

Craig Podmore asserts the moral right

to be identified as the author of this work.

Cover image description: Nancy Spungen death, Chelsea Hotel, 1978

ISBN 978-1-326-61039-5

WWW.AMMOSEXBARBITURATES.COM

TOSSING SALAD

Ghosts live inside here –

Trials of inveterate brutality

Sever bounds of society,

Sex & profanity.

Don't kiss the chrysalis

Until you know what it is…

This is delivering evil

In the form of sanity,

Your sanitary towels

And your flatulent bowels;

Anatomy of vulvas

On crosses,

Sexless.

Kiss a porn star and show me your heart.

Ascend,

Crash

Like heroin-suicide-kings;

They are not things,

Just…misunderstandings.

Denude I

before your camera

and divulge god's reproductive organs in the shape of atrocities.

Now spread your legs and show me your deity, mags full of bullets &

contraceptives, Hamburger Hill in your anal cavity, blunt instruments

as sex toys, a pistol whipped Christ, celibate sex offenders on register
but

that depends on your chequebook…nestle into your modern ways,
displays

of demeaning hellion strays, stigmata misogynists, raping limousines &

grooming in shopping markets i.e. Jamie Bulger, purchasing murders,

murderers purchasing fabric softeners and other domestic
trivialities/Hitler/Hitler

/Hit…her, the disgust, the vile disgust, the unrepentant, Broadmoor

sentiment and political cabinet child sex…this is complex, this complex,
this

is a shopping complex, rare spandex and other lubrications,
manifestations

of nothing in bloodied panties of victims, dormant in Ian Brady/IAN
BRADY/IAN/I AM NOT barbaric, it was an "existential exercise" –
exercise/exorcise/patronise/disguise like whores on mundane tax
supplies…eat your breakfast, that's a good boy NOW GO TO SCHOOL,
LEARN HOW TO DIE & IGNORE THE HOLOCAUST, READ
ABOUT THE FUCKING QUEEN, TELL YOUR MUMMY THAT
YOU SAW A MAN WITH A GUN, INSANE at DUN-FUCKIN'-
BLANE, remnants of breakfast is now on the floor: objects of a bore,
mundane, illicit, complicit in this flesh

consuming system…there's a hole in my chest.

Terrorists - place your marketing scheme here!

Monsters are made here in the U-FUCKIN'-K, &

it's not okay, it's not OK, ok? Ok? 9/11 sexologists;

the day the modern era lost its erection…this is not

THERAPY YOU shit, I eat my cocaine with a spoon not

a fork, you shit, you love tossing salad, we all toss the salad in

our empty souls. Eat ASS AND GET WELL FUCKIN' SOON.

THE CARL PANZRAM POP MUSIC VIDEO

Body ripped. Apart. Cavities fucked. Hell eyes, anus mouth, sex slave flatulence, a fist-fucked cunt angel in hospital robes.

Let's put the fun in funeral. Cock jism breath with gravestone allergies, semen on dead skin, not a single given fuck about it…dead kids, the bruised torso life…guts penetrated…church yard fag butts – skin debris; methods of torture, smell of skin, scum skin, skin of sin, the rage of Dis, disassemble genitalia in the mouth of I, killer rot, blood in baby cot…

born dead or not at all. Reformation: maim, bludgeon, might and rise – hard-on blood craze. Rectum smiles in the gutters. Burp, belch the stench of foetal matter and shit out the remnants of man onto my dinner plate…scoff the fucking lot! Nurtured in hate. It isn't anger, no, just habitual violence.

Fucked in ass, left for dead, eat the soil, this is your death scene, maniacal indifference of your petty suffering, this pain canvas, the lacerations inflicted, you should be grateful you pathetic little boy, stop crying,

your mother isn't missing you, my mother hates me, my father fucked me now I'm fucking you, you menial bastard of arbitrary flesh!

Let's stop for a dance routine, ah, yes, routine, abattoir routine, adept in slaughter, dancers of savagery, the meat of innocence voluptuously molested upon the flesh of beauty, the TV screens breathe misanthropy, they galvanise me, the adulation of barbarity, cool cruelty of popular culture, I'm the face underneath the static, the anthem plays during the orchestration of asphyxiation – this is what you gave birth to, now, smile, pray, pay your bills until I have you by the scruff of the neck; wanton bloodlust and semen,

your serfdom slays me, the fine art of civilisation gives me the amoral right to be the entity that makes you feel…mortal. My cock burns for more rape and brutality, I won't stop, why should I? My only reason for living is to cause suffering of the blind. You can all sing for me like you do in the throes of deathly ecstasy. You make it easy.

However, until the day you're immune to me, allow me to be adored by impunity, you modern men, you make me celebrity as I laugh at your petty mortality upon the gallows, no more fear, instead, you lack empathy

and praise me, sell me, kiss my rotten corpse. I am perplexed.

IAN'S DRINKING CHEAP RED WINE AGAIN...

Ian's drinking that cheap red wine again, cocktails of Nietzsche and Das Rheingold ad infinitum, that human stench, it is profane, the low watt radio hisses the arias whilst Ian fantasises about the final solution, dead Jews stain the hues of his kitsch woodchip wallpaper, that death institute...

"The only way to indulge in freedom is to commit the greatest crime and that is murder."

Knives and photography, grainy black and white realities captured in the psycho eye, amateur narcissist, a sickly aperture, Ian cannot stand this sty, his own existential rhetoric – Sade reigns the rickety coffee table, extinguished cigarettes mount the ash tomb, Ian hates, Ian has thoughts of amoral states, his superiority complex inflates, Ian's drinking that cheap red wine again.

Myra talks about dying her hair, she's singing those Christmas songs again, she's a monstrous, kitsch Marilyn in sin dressed like a typical Christian mother, she doesn't get Nietzsche and she hates the whiny voice on the Wagner record that Ian plays continuously. Poor, explicit nudes of Myra, black and white vulgar martyr, a post-mortem pin-up, a sickly saint veiled in pernicious foul...Ian rants, Ian pervasively increases the atmosphere of drunken dread, Myra laughs, she's fed and fed intellectual disease, Myra doesn't get it but it turns her on, it's his profane enigma.

Myra tries on a new dress, humming the 'pa rum pum pum pum' song, another glass for Ian, same for Myra, they dance like they did on the moors that afternoon, Ian stares at himself in the mirror, gazing wildly like a pious troop of the Gestapo, Myra's friends bore Ian, fashion and hairstyles, newborn babies and guys at work, Ian thinks about the Nuremberg Trials, Goebbels and Eichmann's televised bile, it takes a while to try and adjust to arbitrary chat however, inward and cagey, playing with his knives and sniggering at Myra's old religious books, 'Jesus saves me' and all that bollocks...

Ian wants more cheap red wine...Nazi books, sex toys for an inappropriate target audience; snap shots of victims, private collection – hideous portraits of innocent skin ravished and mutilated, innocent skin marks easier...the little bodies weigh nought, Ian thought to himself; 'my strength; omnipresent like some unwanted god beyond the virtues and serfdom of asinine civilisation...my murderous drive is only natural; it's nothing else but humanity'.

The scars on the moors pervade the erogenous sickness in Ian's perverted ideology, an isolated philosophy born in the depths of Glaswegian urbanism, generating a new man, adopting his vehicle that is flesh and bone, discarding it as trash, a malicious tool to carry out fantasies that could be deemed beyond the pseudo virtues of man...delirious, deleterious intelligence graphically enhanced by the scribes of Sade and Himmler.

What is the microcosm of murder in comparison to the magnitude of war? Murder is allowed in the hands of one that bestows a badge or some faux regalia that honours the protection of the innocent...indifferent, belligerent...Zarathustra in a wheelchair.

"The blood doesn't play games, it's transcendent."

The soil screams, the dew is the sweat that perforated the skin pores of the unfortunate youthful souls in the throes of death, Ian's hands on the glands of babe, little pallid darlings now stare at the black of earth, empty silence, rapacious cuts of night in the frames of sullen, naked miseries wrapped in the cold skeletal fingers of the grass blades, bathing in madness, trauma in the eyes of grain, absorbing the violence, grave of nothing, disturbed dirt; residual, palpable aggression in the ether of winter's depression.

Ian revels in this land of uncivil immortality, negating the wombs of messiah, vetoing the ever-pervasive moral that guides mankind into blindness. More cheap red wine; it pours, the trickling sound like that of a severed neck or a breaking spine, the veins of fluid stick to the sides of the glass – the cries that mournfully stains that audio tape, the tears that fall, just like the wine in that glass, except, it doesn't scream for its mother. Myra is the dregs of the bottle; an empty playground for his little games, thus, when the wine's gone, what else is there?

Murder, of course.

ASBO

Your clitoris
is a psychopath
rummaging for a
god that's extinct
in the eye of her
profane beauty...

DIScard

Perhaps victims

Are love letters

To the void that consumes them.

Their veins dry

In the mouth of earth,

Their bruised windpipes

Are signatures defying

The meaning of identity

And the utter fucking regret

Of being born.

Knell

The quarrel of self has to take place in solitude

So that the predatory state emerges,

The conflicting issues of virtue and animal

Externalises into a bold refrain,

However, the rage and the disdain against

The grain of principles egotistically takes reign;

This godly sadness results in slain

Of another, all because his mother

Prevailed the maniacal truth

Of this brutal creed…

Too much for a little seed, for a little seed hasn't yet seen the sun.

Ochlocracy

Disfigurement is the vulgar effigy of mortality,

Although, not as wretched as evolution,

Its deleterious form only creates wisdom

Of another lie, another prison of thought.

It is, of course, the inveterate malignancy

That is welcoming in the church of

So-called nature...

And in that church,

We scatter,

We fade

And crumble like crispy autumnal leaves.

Ah, yes, spring is most certainly the cruellest season.

Warm beer at 2am…

Corpse rot on my cock,

Feeling sick in my grandma's basement.

Disposing death before mortis,

Inner debates whether to eat them or not.

I can't fit in anywhere.

I can mix with the dead,

They don't think that I'm square.

I should make art out of these guys,

A sculpture of sorts,

An altar of their deathly beauty.

Existence is utterly flawed,

Therefore I enjoy the empty shells

Of victims that replicate the living.

In their murdered smiles

I simulate a friendly conversation,

Often with sexual discourse,

The inanimate structure becomes attractive

In a way like the guys did back in the army.

The anal cavity is looser than it's natural state

But not as moist,

With my pervasive beer-breath stained saliva,

I lubricate it and proceed to fuck it.

The funny thing is,

His face is the same stoic expression

After the blow to his beautiful head:

Emphatic pain

Like the drain

In an abattoir

Of nothing

But sexually flawed persons.

This ennui…

Perhaps I'll eat his genitals later,

I don't know.

Alienation, penetration into the scar of night,

Heterogeneous-erogenous-erroneous sorrow

Unto the fetid discord of my parents' deterioration;

Am I to blame?

This lanky frame of I,

Silently in a rage

That's not accepted within this design,

On this cruel stage.

Getting drunk before work,

Brooding over the cadaver in my living room…

I left the TV on to entertain his mortis-stained eyes,

In the reflection of his porcelain skin

I see myself masturbating

With a frivolous hatred,

Faecal membrane tissue

In my urethra,

Penile death soak fuck,

I relish it but I'm also afraid of it.

I drink my beer next to the vats

That contains the shells of my lovers.

I don't understand loss,

I refrain to emboss my amorality,

Since I impaled that dog's head back when I was a teen,

My curiosity in decomposition was ignited

Like an obscene flame

Within the verbal anxieties of my father's

Compulsive demise.

I cannot chastise the cries of my inner demons –

Depressed at high school,

Automatically canonised into the league

Of unwanted specimens.

In my alcohol malaise,

I dreamt about being powerful

Like the guy in that sci-fi

And Hitler too…

I started to personify,

A manifestation,

An ugly god with a carnivorous appetite,

Drinking youthful semen

From the disenfranchised masses

Of pitiful ruminations.

Defecation delight

In the sterilised light

Of empty bars;

The malnutrition of desire

Wantonly devouring my innards,

I want to suck the sex from him,

Before and after his death.

The sexy-stale-blue skin

In stasis – fellatio bliss,

Acid unto brain,

You are complicit in my world;

My world that is a repugnant cyst

Yet, I accept my choice in this,

It's what makes me feel comfortable in this dimension

That has never accepted me.

There's no sympathy for monsters, no,

I agree with that and for that,

I don't know whether to absorb some sort of gratification for it

Because at least it makes me feel...pertinent.

This unwanted malignance is like puberty –

Bemusing like despair unaware in a lair

Of one's own dirtied and soiled mind;

A mortician's Eros halo,

Blind to the throes of putrification,

Erection for the cloak of Thanatos.

The apartment is starting to smell.

Another can of beer

To adjust to clarity

In this smear of rigid malice.

Perhaps hit the bars again,

I want to find the right man.

His skull has to be pretty.

Anything is pretty in subjugation,

The fecund submission,

The serfdom of mortality

Infuses my reign of being,

Creating progeny of fear and mania.

In this lonely vortex of Milwaukee,

The ubiquitous isolation and factory dust,

The empty beer bottles and insatiate lust

Allows me to indulge beyond what's acceptable.

I'm the physicality of obscenity

Yet, I'm unable to understand that.

My reflection is a silent paroxysm

In duality with extensive pessimism

Discoloured with the blood

Of raw and voluptuous onanism.

All of this impulsive slaughter

Comes from the bowels

And taste of company

Triggered by the aggression of my parents' descent

And deathly curiosities.

From the confounds dispersed from angry mouths

Assimilated by youthful ears,

Discerning interaction to be

Hurtful and asinine –

The recognisable humming of my younger years

Programmed one not to be a part

Of your design.

Perhaps it was my cancerous existence,

Perhaps it was my reluctance,

My repudiation of sincere living.

Another beer.

Heart on stove.

Naked.

The beguiling head in fridge.

Rotting lovers.

Drinking.

Passing out.

Hoping to be taken advantage of.

Stay. Please.

Handcuffs.

Sodomy unto

This lifeless shell.

Ejaculate.

Dissipate.

Elevate

Into my own little dying world,

In this room,

In this pocket of annihilation,

This tomb,

Where even the likes of Lazarus is in a coma.

Online Suicide Videos

Pancreas catharsis,

Sex in crashed cars;

Fucking in Jack The Ripper

Victim locations,

Ejaculating where

Spleen and guts once

Splayed and displayed.

She sucks me off

Before potential online

Suicide videos,

Prurient thoughts devour,

Sloppy insatiate saliva slurps

As blood vacuums from the wrists

That persists to dissipate into the abyss

Of social media loneliness.

She swallows me whole

As a noose cracks another spine.

We're all connected online;

An intimate nexus

Of entropic hurts

And ubiquitous brutalism.

Latent "daddies" bruising asses

Reflect the asinine unawareness

Of the imbecilic masses.

Pre-meditated

Binge watching

Psychotics (pre-spree kill)

Venting about

Their inward souls

Like silent cannibals

Ad nauseum…

The digital audience is hollow.

Their cries unnoticed,

Absorbed by apathetic gods

Unto the ether of perpetual wallow,

Only their scorn and rage to be displayed

In the fragments of aftermath,

No puddle of blood too shallow

Before this pantheon of mad massacres

…but there's laughter and cynicism –

Planting another progeny of psycopathy.

Eric Harris and Dylan Klebold

Fornicating, gyrating with their firearms

Whilst spouting eschatological passages

Inside a pile of hideous entrails that Gein

Discarded upon his kitchen floor.

We take notice of the silence
After the loud, anarchic noise of violence
In the purge of media and lukewarm forms
Of philanthropic condescension.

Inside the selfie cam
Is an isolator – an incubator,
Above the vital organs is
A tumour of inertia;
A vaccinated, well-armoured bubble
Filled with delusional anxieties,
Despairing fantasies
Of self-loathing vanity
And puss inducing
Degradation into the only
Intimate interactions that they know…
Killing.

Although, this is their way of saying;
"Hello. I exist too."

Rape Fantasy

Fundamental beatings

Without empathy;

A dancing welts.

A 34DD bra-scar

In the white of eye.

A blowjob pyre,

Carcinogenic malaise –

Symbolists deface

The veneer of pretty faces

Lit upon the anatomical abomination

Of the urban rape-scape of metropolitan life.

To be truly liberal…is rape fantasy.

Intimacy

This burial ground of semen filled monstrosities

Embalm the façade of being civil;

The abscess of living,

Buying and selling,

Fucking and killing

Seems to be the ingredients

Of materialistic brutality.

Your clothes and possessions

Are the receipts for genocidal expenses.

As you ejaculate into the mouth of an abyss,

Deforms all sacred beauty…

The punctured jaw,

The bullet ridden face

Of a child

Becomes the very nonchalance of your being.

Your credit card ovulates unto the vacuum of blood,

Remains of prostitutes

Distorts your morning coffee like a bad advertisement

For Viagra.

The suit that you bought fits perfectly

Just like Gein's mother's face upon his own.

Lower your crown onto the mound of faecal dirt

Created by the masses of ignoble spenders,

Let the dead whore with cheap suspenders

Ruin your shopping spree,

May your ruminations of social media

Disperse into shattered glass of your self-portrait,

Drenched in the crime scene logistics

Of your lack of intimacy.

Scraps

The rats haven't pissed in her mouth...yet.

It's my possession, my trash

But I like going back to her,

Focusing on her decay,

The degrading face;

The paroxysm of death

In her exposed eye of woe

That mirrors the very struggle

That we had –

Every erotic wince, every arousing throe...

It was a heated altercation,

I had my member ready,

I trembled with anguish

And could not keep her steady.

Head trauma, a bleeding silence;

Now, that enabled me to perform on her,

The stasis of death in its immaculate, conceptual imperfection

Made me ejaculate into her sweet, chaste chasm

Amidst debris of rubbish and piss stained concrete.

No dead spiders in her mouth…yet.

She was so sweet.

So upsetting that such benevolence

Has to be defiled in the face of adversity.

Scraps of old butchered meat

Sticks to her stagnant ceramic-hard skin,

Lamb chop bones, broccoli,

Dog foul and other banal remnants

Of refuse attach to her;

A metastasizing malaise

Of cum stench games

And post-vigour violence

Proliferated by the ugly

Of discord and delusional,

Visceral rage.

I want to eat her passport photo.

I want to eat the family photo

And then spit it out,

Half eaten, next to her corpus.

The ants haven't nested within her mouth…yet.

That gutted pig;

The putrefaction manifested

Into the maelstrom of my guts,

The wretch of lust

And carnivore dreams of vaginal thrust,

Not a shred of her shall be wasted!

The lascivious abattoir

Gave me meaning

In its scraps of tainted flesh.

This prurient, nameless alleyway

Adjacent to my neighbour's gutter

Satisfies me, spilling seeds into its melancholic frame

In the spit of torpid rain,

The arbitrary trickle of water

Perpetuates the ignorance of malignance

In this infinitesimal corner of earth,

This little pocket of pain

Like a broken void

Separate from the sections of acceptable living.

The nocturnal scavengers haven't nibbled on her face...yet.

Ah, the nil of it.

Wait for another human to come across

This abhorrence and watch them discern

Every inch of death with questions

And asinine hypotheses; they just theorise.

Does a caterpillar ever stop to define the demise of butterflies?

Toilet Mouth

Kissing Christ with condom lips…

Procreation in the turd of blindness,

The deepest fathom of shit

And raped cunt salivates in an atom

That grows after every violent blow,

It inflates after a bleeding lip,

It pulsates in the adrenaline of forced sodomy –

The autonomy of amorality

Bequeathed by disabled disciples

In an organism gorging the sweat

Off of a holocaust orgasm.

Lie naked for me,

Disengage, despondence,

Reclaim rage from the slumber

Of inertia and proceed

To cut off your genitalia

In the name of the state.

A faceless prostitute

Destitute in remnants of Syria

Eats the rubble as well as the cocks

Of thousands of armed men.

Ejaculate and faeces in a piss bowl

Full of disposed waste and

Tiny foetuses.

Forget the flush,

Let it stagnate,

Let it mingle and become

The new universe of pain;

A void of antipathy

And aberrations for

Parades of inveterate consumers.

Pontius Pilate discerns the courts

Of hysteria and torn hymen,

Setting alight to blank semen

In the oceans of stoical media martyrs.

Forcing open this toilet mouth

With soiled dentures and oral vices

To allow the feral bureaucrats

To purge the abdominal blood of innocents

Into the depths of its excremental denizens.

At the very bottom, beyond the cycle of whores,

Who are systematically licking clean the rim of this

Shit infested veneer of true apathy,

Spores of authoritarians with prolapsed halos

Hum their ignoble national anthems

And torture chamber devices shaped like

A manger and stables, moral fables

That obfuscates the liberal and able.

Mass productions of Dolmance,

Dominations of autocratic libidos

For the populous who happen to be on their knees,

Hissing like injured serpents in an abyss

Of sepulchral clarity and corrupt governing bodies

Copulating each other in the midst of

Genocidal erotica and witch trial despot mobs

With penetrable tools to infiltrate insatiate

Sexual wounds.

There is no good.

There is no bad.

Just shit, piss and that obvious mistake

Called man.

Semen Samples Found in The Throat of a Deceased Subject

Predatory little lukewarm gods in the trashcans that contain the heads of lovers…adultery, bestial fuckers, blood around their mouths like handicapped butchers…sandpapered lips of cunt, pubic hair wrapped in cellophane, discarded statues of saints – desecrated, humiliated and headless (replaced by booty call numbers translated in a false Aramaic)…next to the gutter, abandoned prams in the process of erosion, girls with stained glass eyes play with dolls with heads for knives…alleyways for the disenfranchised; condescending assimilation in disguise, emphatically emphasised by the cum-rot that is modern man:

"The disenfranchised? From what and whom are they disenfranchised from exactly? Where did they all belong in the first place?"

Discarded tissues from the guts of a peep show…piss pots containing skull fragments and skin waste in the nostrils of the alienated, injured war vets like blisters on the nowhere shore but somewhere in the caw-like vocals of a molested whore there are food banks, such good charity in the clarity of adversity; what a stale mess in the puss of free bread and milk, blessed are we, we have to exist, we have to soil ourselves, admit and confess that we're nothing but repugnant and worthless society fillers like pointless scenes in a silent film left on the cutting room floor.

Let the noble gland of the rapacious psychotic dressed in opulence cum in our throats, such mere and bland debris we are, sexual wheelie bins – numb, ashen, divulging the sodomy, the sewer graves allow us to dissipate into the masturbatory deaths, cadaverous blow-up dolls witnessing more abuse unto the stasis of post-mortem…colonoscopy unto the skies of feral urges, voluptuous bloodied fist in the mouths of missing persons…the slippage of skin on newly trimmed lawns, a broken tooth embedded into the salacious flesh of an amputated stripper; the arbitrary numbness of killings, clear regression on talk shows recorded for the silence of the future, the tragic Aprils and Millys fading into the monotony of the everyday life procedure…scars and colostomy bags full of profane prayers, decapitated head, traces of semen…

…time of death: uncertain.

Straightjacket Symphony

Rosemary West's breasts

Better than Oppenheimer's atom bomb tests.

Sullen fucking and a crying orgasm

In the cellar

Where children play dead.

Eat the fabric of coffin lids,

Watch the films of Anatoly Slivko

Before ordering overpriced coffees to go.

Post-Soviet hammer games

To feed the ennui of desolation.

Physical digression of homicide,

Emptiness is the altar of matricide and patricide,

Exemplifying the perfect nuclear family

In oral sex positions,

Sucking the insides!

Pests shaped like razor blades

In the darker shades of my mind;

Dialysis of delusion,

Narcissistic infusion

Protrudes imagery of the humiliated dead.

Lovers unite in the plight of lust

Gone too far like Sid and fucking Nancy,

Jaw ajar, a mauled bra on dead meat,

Disposed of,

Addicts itching and antsy

Kissing mass-produced plastic Christ feet

For the necromancy of their own selfish solitude.

Syringe hole pariahs

On a pale horse

Unto the beyond of fetid

World scourge.

This,

Delusional parasitosis

Is just letting you know that you exist

Under the restraints

Of the virtuous insignificants.

Charles Starkweather,

An adept applicant

For this commode

Of recalcitrant needs.

The revolver is where the heart is,

The toilet flush however,

Resides in your conscience.

Kraft-Ebing

Cleavage,

Slit ankles in cold water,

Corset-feral-baby,

The disposed faecal matter –

Fecund mediocre fellatio,

Cuckold bitch drinking urine,

Coprophagy urges,

Standard striptease

Before a shallow grave of stars

And heterosexuals under the bed sheets;

Missionary ennui

In a suburban bedroom,

Copulation,

Condom,

Time to dissipate,

Can't ejaculate...

Socialite

In bulimic fashion,

Disembowelled in torn lingerie

For the disfigured lens –

The venerable mistress with

The perfume of corporate death

Deepens the loathing of others

To the state of implacable disintegration.

Reformation, only in the shade

Of her nude contours;

Denuding the suffering

For the laughter of

Tabloid executioners.

She's missile-anorexic-bile

Designed in middle class isolation…

Supreme apathy in the pineal form of wanton lust,

Garters, ass, legs and bust!

She performs webcam shows

In the Arras memorial,

Local abattoirs,

Abandoned death campsites

And job centres that smell of a damp depression

Amidst whiffs of cheap coffee and

Incontinent perspiration.

Her ballistics

Littered with war zone wounds

And human fragmentation.

The soft, pulpy and grey tissue

She stabs cold-heartedly with her stomping stilettos

Below her majestic anatomy

Is the surface of truth she loves to deny;

Death and abject despondence

Is her cruel yet beatific

Rise to narcissistic omnipotence,

That is her repulsive pride, her belief.

She downs a glass of champagne

And wipes her mouth of entrails

With an expensive handkerchief.

Drag The Body

Pseudo martyrs of the wretched

Sing ills to the constant hum of modernity.

The misguided and regressed

Bow to the inevitable onslaught,

Their triviality threatened

By cruelty of the absurd;

The catechism created by grain of thought,

From the seed of man

Into the spire of the bullet

That turns all into rapacious thugs.

The advancing epistemology rages on,

Developing into buffoonery

And primordial ineptitude.

Conscience deforms and salivates

In the face of civil passivity,

Rupturing conformity, obeying the death of what we don't understand.

So, let's drag this body,

This overweight vulgarity

To the nearest shallow grave and

Apply the dirt to its abominable face.

Hide the documents that noted its existence.

Burn all Polaroids of its nudity

And disabled infants…

This body is derogatory,

The body is a vile pouch of past

Reflecting in a tear of future,

The wealth of violence

Is perpetually in abundance

In its pale jaws of time

That erases within every stir.

Drag this body,

Drag the body,

Drag…

There's No Chemical Castration for Thought

Pre-pubescent vessel

Galvanised in the shadows

Of the malnourished;

Inveterate sadists

Eat neighbourhoods

And humanitarians,

Evading exposure

Of their unwise appetite –

The culmination of

Detached worlds,

Accessing their own morality

In the faces of

Sad little girls.

Natural Selection

Remove the membrane upon the eye of the world, strip back the film, cut the organ, let it fart out the last pockets of gas…laugh at its seizure, ridicule its powerlessness, belittle its pathetic little pulse, prod its uterus, mirror the world unto its foetal eye…spread its legs and apply the vacuum of viscera.

Tickle the sensual lips, it discharges hate, lubricates a vacancy; the progeny becomes its own executioner: the membrane now covers the face of its killer.

Printed in Great Britain
by Amazon